CONSTELLATION ROUTE

CONSTELLATION
ROUTE

MATTHEW OLZMANN

Alice James Books
FARMINGTON, MAINE
alicejamesbooks.org

10 9 8 7 6 5 4 3 2 1

Alice James Books are published by Alice James Poetry Cooperative, Inc.,
an affiliate of the University of Maine at Farmington.

Alice James Books
114 Prescott Street
Farmington, ME 04938
www.alicejamesbooks.org

Library of Congress Cataloging-in-Publication Data

Names: Olzmann, Matthew, author.
Title: Constellation route : poems / Matthew Olzmann.
Description: Farmington, ME : Alice James Books, [2022]
Identifiers: LCCN 2021010024 (print) | LCCN 2021010025 (ebook) | ISBN
    9781948579230 (trade paperback) | ISBN 9781948579476 (epub)
Subjects: LCGFT: Poetry.
Classification: LCC PS3615.L96 C66 2022 (print) | LCC PS3615.L96 (ebook)
    | DDC 811/.6--dc23
LC record available at https://lccn.loc.gov/2021010024
LC ebook record available at https://lccn.loc.gov/2021010025

Alice James Books gratefully acknowledges support from individual donors,
private foundations, the University of Maine at Farmington, the National
Endowment for the Arts, and the Amazon Literary Partnership. Funded in
part by a grant from the Maine Arts Commission, an independent state agency
supported by the National Endowment for the Arts.

Cover art: Golden boy / 2012, digital 3d, Adam Martinakis

CONTENTS

TWO

THREE

FOUR

FOR VIEVEE

Neither snow nor rain nor heat nor gloom of night stays these couriers
from the swift completion of their appointed rounds.

—HERODOTUS

I shook from my pockets
withered letters, litter, leaves not addressed to me.

—WISŁAWA SZYMBORSKA

Day Zero

The date when a mailpiece enters the mailstream and the date when
the clock starts for purposes of service performance measurement.
—*United States Postal Service, "Glossary of Postal Terms"*

The old man in the old house yells, *Let there be light,*
then flicks a switch on the living room wall
to watch the house come to life. He looks up, pleased
with his joke and claps his hands. He says,
Let the water under the sky be gathered to one place,
as he twists a steel knob, and the sea washes over
the dishes in his sink. Let there be bookcases,
couches, a table made of oak. Let there be oolong
in the kettle, a black molly in the aquarium,
and a photo album to hold memories of the dead.
Loneliness. Quietude. Leaves falling in the front yard
and no one to talk to. Suddenly, it's not so delightful,
and the man slumps into a rocking chair. He wants
to tell you about this place, this world he's conjured
while sleeping. He writes your name on his favorite
stationery. Seals the envelope. Walks to the mailbox
at the end of the street. Tomorrow, he'll do this again,
but bigger, grander, more expensive. This is no
Genesis, which starts on the first day. More like
a dress rehearsal, the day before. Day Zero.
The letter is in the mail. When it reaches you,
everything begins.

ONE

Letter to Bruce Wayne

—After Borges

A good place to hide a drop of water is a stream.
A good place to hide a stream is beneath an ocean.

A good place to hide a man is among thousands
of men. Watch how they rush
through the city like water through a ravine.

I've searched many famous cities for you.
There are three listings for "Bruce Wayne"
in Houston, two in Pittsburgh, one in Miami, and one in LA.

In Tampa, Bruce Wayne is a retired chemistry teacher.
In Flagstaff, he drives a taxi and hopes
to procure a diamond for his soon-to-be fiancée.

A good place to hide a star is a galaxy.
A good place to hide a galaxy is a universe.
Look at the night sky. Justice

used to be a cowl and cape, the flicker
of wings under an etiolated moon. And you,
like a gargoyle, crouched atop some stone edifice.

To conceal a universe, place it in a multiverse—that hypothetical
klatch of alternate realities. The dilemma of the word

alternate is how it implies a norm, a progenitor stream
from which the alternate diverges. Which is the alternate?
Which is right here, right now? There is no such thing

as Gotham City, but here is Gotham City and I've been
so naïve: believing the truth of the old mythologies.
How they promised a recognizable villain,
a clown with a ruby-slashed mouth, a lunatic's laugh.

In the universe where I exist, supervillains
look like everyone else. Give them an old flannel
to wear and a square jawline to smile at the world.

They're hanging a noose in a middle school bathroom.
They're shouting, *Get out of my country*,
from the window of a passing car.
They're pulling a pistol in a crowded barroom,
or bus stop, or the middle of the street.
They could be anyone. They could be everywhere.

A good place to hide a sociopath is a full-length mirror.
A good place to hide that mirror is the heart of America.

In the battle of Good versus Evil, I was so sure
Good would win. Now I just hope something Good will survive,
get a job cutting hair or selling cars, make it home for dinner.

I suspect there's a parallel dimension where you, Vigilante,
long for this as well. To have a normal life is victory enough.
To remain anonymous and not be spat upon on the subway.

In Boston, Bruce Wayne owns a pawn shop.
In Milwaukee, he plays pinochle and feeds stray cats.
In New Hampshire, he goes fly-fishing on the Sugar River,
reels in one brook trout after another.

When he removes the hook from a mouth,
he might place the fish in a cooler.
Or, he might set it back into a stream—
the alternate or the original—no longer certain
in which he stands.

Letter to the Horse You Rode in on

From this day forth, let it be understood: as one
of God's most graceful innovations, you—
dear horse—are entitled to certain provisions
under the law. Granted, the law is one
I just made up, but those who acknowledge
its validity will adhere to the following rule:
One does not, under any circumstance, say "fuck you"
to a horse. It matters not who rode in on
the aforementioned steed. It matters not
what kind of jackassery said rider has committed.
We shall not allow even the tangential fuck you
to be cast upon this virtuous and sophisticated being,
such as the fuck-you-by-association commonly
phrased as: *Fuck you and the horse you rode in on.*
No, dear horse, you are proof that one does not
have the luxury of choosing the burden
one carries. Fate makes an animal of us all, and rides us
through the village at sunrise where we are judged.
But we designed those villages. We built them
from our worst ideas and kept expanding until
each enclave was equipped with genetically modified
pigeons and flammable tap water. The human hand
can reach from one ruined thing to the next. It can
throw a whiskey bottle against a wall, drive a car
into a ditch, wave good-bye. It can run its fingers
through your mane, and if I find you, I will
say: *You would've done a better job with this place.*
Unfortunately, horses don't have any say in governance.
Except once. It's said that the emperor Caligula,

nominated his horse, Incitatus, as a Roman Consul.
We should also note: Caligula's reign was brief.
37-41 AD. Then he was slain.

Letter Written While Waiting in Line at Comic Con

Klingon, Parseltongue, Na'vi.
People invent imaginary languages so imaginary
citizens of imaginary worlds can speak
to one another. Elvish, Ewokese,
Dothraki. You can learn these languages,
come to a convention with your face painted blue
or a leather scabbard bolted to your back,
and talk to people who will understand you.
I understand what language feels like
when you're not understood. More than once,
I thought some other planet might be my home.
Last week, in an alley, I saw a man punch another man
until neither looked like a person.
There are hundreds of reasons like this
to long to be from some other galaxy,
century, or dimension. Reasons
to put on a space suit or wizard's cloak
and hope no one will recognize you. But it's not
these costumes that amaze me; it's always been
the languages. The way they reach
for something that can't be said
in our tongue. In the only language I know,
there are not enough words for *parabola*
or *isotope*. Too few phrases to say *I'm*
sorry or *I'm glad that I found you.*

Though we've been married for years,
I wish we met when we were children.
If we had known each other in the year

you spent alone on Earth without one friend,
we could've been aliens together.
I'd have those green, four-fingered hands.
You, with your glow-in-the-dark antennae.
Words in the form of strange whirling noises.
Low chirping machine music.
Wisps of static, lamentations of rain.
Only you and I would know what these sounds meant

The First Official Post Office of the American Colonies (1639)

Less of an office, more like some guy's house.

Also, it serves as a pub, and the pub

(which has a certified license to serve *stronge water*)

is likely a better business than the mail.

Welcome to Richard Fairbanks' Tavern.

This is Boston, Black Jack Alley, and the mail carrier

is any traveler who trundles toward the next town.

As in, *You're going to Marblehead? Can you take this?*

And if the answer is *Yes*, it will get there

in a few weeks or maybe a couple months.

And by *get there*, I mean it will end up

in another tavern, inn, or brothel.

Wait. You're sending this letter overseas?

Even worse. Make six copies and place them

on six different ships. Pray.

I too have longed for the stronge water.

I too have sent my six fastest ships

and heard nothing in response.

How impossible is this: to reach across time

or oceans to say the one thing you need to say?

And if a parcel is sent for you,

good luck knowing when it arrives.

Let's say it's from your aunt,

but your aunt can't spell your name,

none of the drunks here know who you are,

and the barkeep is reading your mail.

Letter to the Person Who, During the Q&A Session after the Reading, Asked for Career Advice

The confusion you feel is not your fault.
When we were younger, guidance counselors steered us
toward respectable occupations: doctor, lawyer,
pharmacist, dentist. Not once did they say exorcist,
snake milker, or racecar helmet tester.
Always: investment banker, IT specialist, marketing associate.
Never: rodeo clown.
Never: air guitar soloist, chainsaw
juggler, or miniature golf windmill maker.
In this country, in the year I was born,
some 3.1 million other people were also born, each
with their own destiny, the lines of their palms
predicting an incandescent future. Were all of them
supposed to be strategy consultants and commodity analysts?
Water slide companies pay people to slide down
water slides to evaluate their product.
Somehow, that's an actual job. So is naming nail polish colors.
Were these ever presented as options?
You need to follow your passion
as long as your passion is not poetry and is definitely a hedge fund.
If I could do it over, I'd suggest an entry level position
standing by a riverbank,
or a middle management opportunity
winding like fog through the sugar maples of New England.
There's a catastrophic shortage
of bagpipe players, tombstone sculptors and tightrope walkers.
When they tell you about the road ahead,
they forget the quadrillion other roads.

You'll know which one is yours because
it fills you with astonishment or ends with you being reborn
as an alpine ibex—a gravity-defying goat, able to leap
seven feet in the air, find footholds where none exist,
and (without imagining it could ever be anything else)
scale a vertical sheet of solid rock
to find some branches, twigs, or wild berries to devour.

Letter to Matthew Olzmann from Cathy Linh Che on Saintlinesss

Hi Matthew. Cathy here. I've been thinking
about saintliness and how your great aunt
who lived somewhere in Spain
was beatified to be a saint
and how your Filipino grandmother
told you that saintliness isn't inherited;
it's something you have to earn yourself.
As we contemplate sea rise and California
wildfires devouring the forests
and oil spillage into the very water source
that the people of Standing Rock need to live,
it's hard to think about the afterlife.
What kind of place is that? Maybe it's
a house among the Blue Ridge
Mountains where Vievee made Texas-style chili,
read my Tarot, and talked about a bear crossing
the front porch. Maybe it's your one bedroom
apartment filled with books, above
a coffee shop in Detroit. (Thanks for letting us stay.)
I think about the shores of Hội An where
I've hurled myself into the ocean, twice,
as a baptism into a country my parents
once considered home. No one in my family
has ever been beatified to be a saint,
but the Vietnamese have 117 martyrs, which
we pride ourselves on. I think about dying
for a religion introduced to my father's family
by the colonizing French. Or a religion

that beat the Oglala language from Lakota schoolchildren
in South Dakota. I'll never be a saint.
I won't die for anyone,
not the way religion has taught me,
not the way Prince has sung.
All I have are the words I'm writing to you,
which I hope, friend, are good enough.

Letter to the Oldest Living Longleaf Pine in
North America

—Southern Pines, NC

I expected a God, a titan
towering above the rest of the forest. Instead,
you were only a tree.
Not a sequoia or redwood with their legendary torsos,
thick as the stone turrets of another continent's
medieval castles. Just a regular tree.
An unusually tall and dignified tree, certainly,
but also one with a bend in the spine like a thin man with a bad back.
Fragile. Limping toward some medicated tomorrow.
You looked exhausted. And who wouldn't?
After outliving centuries of witch trials and slave ships,
genocides and confederacies,
logging industries and men from Maryland
sent to harvest your sap for turpentine.
468 years is a long time when,
at any given moment,
someone like me could toss
a cigarette butt from the window of a minivan.
And just like that: history
is an ash-whitened field,
a twenty-square-mile arc of unremarkable flatness
in a space where some ancient breathing things
once stood (the way I now stand), their limbs
stretching to feel the wind weave
through their fingers and branches.

Letter to a Cockroach, Now Dead and Mixed into a Bar of Chocolate

Regulations allow for, on average, sixty insect fragments
per hundred grams of chocolate
in America. You are pulverized.
Your thorax, head, and legs that no longer twitch.
Invisible and milk-smooth.
Nothing harbors a secret like sweetness.

Centuries ago, the Sirens understood
this statute. Each sank their knowledge
inside a voice of chimes and kisses,
hiding the ocean's stone teeth
in a mouth of mist and foam.

Last week, waves beat against a dock in Brazil.
The quick bodies of you and your buddies
quivered across the cargo of cacao beans.
You couldn't possibly comprehend: the beans
on their way to the grinder, just as those ancient sailors
couldn't envision—beyond the Sirens' music—
the broken mast, the shattered hull.

Today is Valentine's Day. I walk to the store
to buy a box of chocolates for my wife.
As I walk, I have no idea whose hands
made the shoes that hug my feet,
or why the fruit at the supermarket
glows like numbers on the stock exchange.

There is sweetness in this world,
but it has a price. You are the price.

Letter to William Shatner

1.

Dear William, I was hoping to talk to you about the time I first saw the movie version of *Fight Club*. If you haven't seen it, it's about young men who punch each other in the face, urinate in the food of strangers, and blow things up. Basically: a documentary. This is their response to the problem of contemporary masculinity, though when said like this, it sounds illogical. Made sense at the time. But there was one scene, where Brad Pitt and Edward Norton's characters discussed who they'd fight if they could fight any celebrity, living or dead. Edward Norton said, *Shatner. I'd fight William Shatner.* Everyone in the audience laughed. But I wasn't sure why.

2.

I too live in a movie where the men are always angry. They're revving their engines and spitting from the windows. Cracking their knuckles and glaring. Burning like flares on a stretch of abandoned highway. They clean their fingernails on the point of a buck knife. Going outside and kicking the dirt. Thinking of their mothers, then yelling at the sky. That sort of thing.

3.

For the past 45 minutes, I've been on hold with Priceline's customer service. I'm being transferred again, to someone who, again, will not be able to explain why my flight reservation which is eligible for cancellation is not actually eligible for cancellation. Every so often, a recording of your voice— dear William Shatner, dear company spokesperson—interrupts the music to tell me that the world's fastest roller coaster is Kingda Ka. To say you'll stay on hold with me. To offer a recitation of a poem you wrote about a woman named Ruth.

4.

Out in the world, men are shouting. Gathering on their sidewalks and shouting. Marching through the streets and shouting. Punching their pals in the ear and shouting. It's how we say things like, *I have the happy feeling,* and also things like, *Every cogent analysis of masculine irrationality determines that its manifestation is more of an ontological inevitability than an innoxious aberration.*

5.

Still on hold with Priceline. And, for an eighth or tenth time, your voice comes in to say, *The world's fastest roller coaster is Kingda Ka.* And by now, I'm saying, *Jesus Christ, can you stop with this already?* Then you offer, again, to share a poem you wrote. And I'm yelling, *No! Just let me talk to a human.* Which is when you actually begin to recite the poem, saying, *There was a young lady named Ruth*—and suddenly I understand: Shatner. *I'd fight William Shatner.*

6.

And just like that: I'm part of the problem. I've punched my card and am back in the He-Man-Spontaneous-Combustion-of-Wrath Society, pacing my living room and shouting. Pressing the phone against my head and shouting. Pounding a fist on the table and shouting. A portable inferno for one, a singularity at the center of the town causing everything to fold inward, all the pipes to rupture, all the buildings to crumble. The men gather around it to holler into the wreckage.

7.

I should say, I don't really want to fight you. Or anyone. That I'm embarrassed by rage, particularly when it's mine, the ordinariness of it. Three strangers, one after another, all trying to fix a problem over the phone, a problem that—like most of my problems—was probably my fault to begin with. There are good people out there. And they fix it. They correct the problem, cancel the flight, and tell me to have a pleasant evening.

8.

The town is quiet, and the streets have now emptied. As if all the shouting men caught a brief glimpse of themselves and, startled by their reflections, ran out of things to yell about. Rethinking their lives, perhaps they've gone home, to rest in moonlit rooms, to light lavender-scented candles, to recline against pillows that cradle the shapes of their fragile heads, to dream of soft hands touching their weathered faces.

9.

The world's fastest roller coaster is Kingda Ka. I know this because you told me. But I've since looked it up. It's named after a 500-pound Bengal tiger. The males of the species are territorial and aggressive, renowned for their teeth, their claws, and their fury. They rip things apart. They are beautiful, but they spend much of their lives alone and are nearly extinct.

Letter Beginning with Two Lines by Czesław Miłosz

You whom I could not save
Listen to me.

Can we agree Kevlar
backpacks shouldn't be needed

for children walking to school?
Those same children

also shouldn't require a suit
of armor when standing

on their front lawns, or snipers
to watch their backs

as they eat their lunches.
They shouldn't have to stop

to consider the speed
of a bullet or how it might

reshape their bodies. But
one winter, back in Detroit,

I had one student
who opened a door and died.

It was the front
door to his house, but

it could have been any door,
and the bullet could have written

any name. The shooter
was thirteen years old

and was aiming
at someone else. But

a bullet doesn't care
about aim, it doesn't

distinguish between
the innocent and the innocent,

and how was the bullet
supposed to know this

child would open the door
at the exact wrong moment

because his friend
was outside and screaming

for help. Did I say
I had *one* student who

opened a door and died?
That's wrong.

There were many.
The classroom of grief

had far more seats
than the classroom for math

though every student
in the classroom for math

could count the names
of the dead.

A kid opens a door. The bullet
Couldn't possibly know,

nor could the gun, because
guns don't kill people, they don't

have minds to decide
such things, they don't choose

or have a conscience,
and when a man doesn't

have a conscience, we call him
a psychopath. This is how

we know what type of assault rifle
a man can be,

and how we discover
the hell that thrums inside

each of them. Today,
there's another

shooting with dead
kids everywhere. It was a school,

a movie theater, a parking lot.
The world

is full of doors.
And you, whom I cannot save,

you may open a door

and enter a meadow, or a eulogy.
And if the latter, you will be

mourned, then buried
in rhetoric.

There will be
monuments of legislation,

little flowers made
from red tape.

What should we do? We'll ask
again. The earth will close

like a door above you.
What should we do?

And that click you hear?
That's just our voices,

the dead bolt of discourse
sliding into place.

Letter to a Bridge Made of Rope—

To the shepherd herding his flock
through the gorge below, it must appear as if I walk
on the sky. I feel that too: so little between me

and The Fall. But this is how faith works its craft.
One foot set in front of the other, while the wind
rattles the cage of the living and the rocks down there

cheer every wobble; your threads keep
this braided business almost intact saying: *Don't worry.*
I've been here a long time. You'll make it across.

TWO

Psychopomp

The new dark of evening, and when the Post Office
closes for the night, it's conceivable the workers
pat each other on the back, punch out, go home.

Or maybe they host rituals of ambergris and ashes, dancing
nymphs, a sacrificed lamb. Could happen. Not likely, but how
do we know? The doors are bolted. The windows, shuttered.

The floor could unlock to reveal a corridor to the underworld.
The job of the psychopomp was to usher souls from here
to there. Usually, they were horses, ravens, nightjars,

angels, or dogs. Famous psychopomps: Mercury, Turms,
and Hermes. Messenger gods. Yes, your mail
is being sorted. But other enterprises are underway as well.

Jung suggested the psychopomp as a bridge
between the conscious and unconscious worlds. My last
therapist found my unconscious world to be a disaster.

Not too different from the actual world with its bruised mouth
and nervous twitching. Glow-in-the-dark livestock. Credit
cards to pay off lesser credit cards. Tires that float in river moss.

Let me tell you about this dream I have where everyone
I love floats out to sea on a ramshackle raft. No oars, no sails,
and I can never save them! Wait—

                                        what was I saying again?

A bridge. Two worlds. The Post Office is dark.
And beneath it all, a messenger god might usher the lost
through a shadow. When he returns, it will be dawn.

Doors will open. Customers will tumble forth.
Stamps and twine, love letters and invoices. Death notices.
Tax forms. Anxiety, anxiety. Personalized stationery.

Letter to David James

I was thinking about your classroom
from almost two decades ago, and how you
tried to explain the theater convention
of addressing characters who were unseen
and offstage. These days, the theater gets dark early
and I'm always talking to someone beyond
the curtain, someone who might not be there.

Have you read Merwin's *Present Company*
or Koch's *New Addresses*? Both are full of such
moments. Speakers speaking directly to things
that are never going to answer: A thief
in the airport, World War II, sleep,
the word yes. There's a question I keep
coming back to in *New Addresses*, the speaker asking:
If this is the way the world ends, is it really going to?

I'm not sure how, exactly, that poem's author
thought the world would end,
but I look around and think if *this*
is the way the world ends—a wall at the border,
presidential tantrums, lead in your drinking water,
and—

I too, might reach out to something that never
answers. For example, God. But why stop with
that inevitable silence? We should talk
to the dead while we're at it, and the trees,
the year 1996, my father's medical history, estranged

citizens quarreling in dislocated corners of the globe,
rusting truck beds, the moon above my neighborhood—

my neighborhood suddenly quiet, the sidewalk now empty
except for me. I've grown comfortable
with the hush that answers each question, how it lingers
above the streetlights as if slung over a hook:

like my pea coat back home, how it hangs in the foyer,
full of nerves and apprehension,
and this body no longer there to wear it.

Questions for Matthew Olzmann from Jessica Jacobs about Imposter Syndrome among the Thorns and Thistles

How old were you, Matthew, when the world tipped
its hand? When things you thought were natural
showed their seams? I was thirteen. On trucked-in pallets
across the street, squares of scutch grass
were stacked high as my head. Did you know a lawn
could be delivered? I didn't. But lured by promises
of Pepsi and pizza, of doing equal work with the boys,
I hauled and placed, puzzling them neat
as a sheet of graph paper.

                    The girls that year had begun
to paint their faces, a line of cheap orange stark
along their jaws. Unlike me, they had not yet learned the art
of how to blend: all those boys I pretended to like; all the girls
I pretended not to. In thrift stores, we tried on others'
past-season selves—the clothes, like the kids in the hallways,
grouped by color and type. We wore masks of slang and song lyrics,
dropped band names like currency, smoked skunk weed
copped from an older brother's underwear drawer. Mirrors held
a special magnetism: instead of homework, I studied myself.

And after school, I walked past the grass, the contrived
squares busy stitching and joining into a lawn, passing
themselves off like they'd been there all along. Yet I could still
feel the weight of that sod, the wet itch of it on my skin, the wonder
that wherever I set it, it would bind itself
to the ground below.

All day, my neighbors' sprinklers stuttered
rainbows. All night, to the hiss of their groundwater whispers,
I traced out my new hips and new breasts, the possibilities
I might grow into.

And now, decades on, I'm trying to grow a lawn
on me, transplanting the tradition
of my ancestors. Heavy with questions, I zip
myself into Judaism like a patchwork parka
of grass, hoping it might take hold, might
grow to fit snug as a golf course greenway.

Matthew, I wish you'd been around then
to ask: outside, the lawn; inside, me: each carefully constructed
as a Lego set, yet also a living breathing dying thing. Were both fake
just because I'd helped make them?

And now, what do you think
of this whole religion thing? Will faith always gape
like a borrowed coat? If something isn't natural can it still be true?

Letter to Justin, Age Seven, Regarding Any Possible Mixed-Race Anxieties Which One Might Experience in the Near or Distant Future

Sometimes, when people talk about white people,
exactly one half of me hits the Eject Button.
Not being white, that half says, *Okay, this thing isn't about me*
so, I'm just going to hang out over there and think about other things,
and then the other half of me tries to tag along,
looks for an exit door he too can slip through,
but the half of me that just opted out, says, *No. This*
is important for you to hear. You really need to sit and listen to this,
and then the other half says, *No, I'm with you. We're*
the same person, and then the first one yells
something like, *Not this time, Colonizer!*
but that's when I notice I'm talking aloud
and everyone's looking at me. It's okay
if everyone's looking at you. It's fine if both voices
are right. If both voices are wrong. If they're not
talking about you but you should listen
because it's important. If they are talking about you
but you shouldn't listen because they're clueless.
You might walk through many rooms.
You were welcome before you arrived.
It's okay if what you feel is anxious.
If what you feel is calm. If what you feel is jarring.
If what you feel can best be described
as torsion pendulums, elm trees,
feeder roots, escrima sticks, algae on the surface
of water surrounding you and then letting you go.
Metaphors link the known and unknown,

the real and imaginary, and they exist
because there are things we have no words for.
It's okay to not have words and,
in their absence, become a bridge. I didn't care
about metaphors when I was your age.
What I cared about then was simple:
convincing my parents to let me have a dog.
That was what was important, and I felt
it was the thing that could best complete my life.
I couldn't have a dog because my mom was allergic.
That is a trait I did not inherit from her.
That is also a metaphor. We don't choose
what we inherit. I did not get a dog.
Instead I got a goldfish.
The goldfish was boring and died after a month
and, really, it doesn't add much
to my narrative. This would be a better story
if I just left that part out. But that's how stories work:
you choose what to include, what's important,
and what belongs to you. You choose how to tell it.
The thing I would tell next
is that I later got a pet salamander. It was beautiful
and weird looking and belonged to both
earth and water. Some salamanders are poisonous.
Some mythologies say they're made from fire.
Some have gills. Some have lungs.
Some have neither and have evolved
to breathe forever through their skin.

Fourteen Letters to a 52-Hertz Whale

1.

Dear 52-Hertz Whale: Because you sing at a frequency no other whales can hear, scientists have nicknamed you *The World's Loneliest Whale*. I'm sure it's unbearable out there, swimming through eternity, calling out and calling out and calling out and calling out and never getting a reply, never hearing a kind word in response.

Wherever you are, I hope you're being careful.

2.

Dear 52-Hertz: Would it be weird if I came to the ocean to visit? I haven't figured out the logistics of this, but it'd be cool to hang for a while. The problem is, I don't know how to find you. I could get to the beach, but then what? If I swam out to meet you, I'd get eaten by tiger sharks. If you swam to the shore, you'd get stuck and die. Once, there was a video going around the internet of a beached whale, and it was dead and the villagers didn't know how to get rid of the carcass. So they tried to blow it up with a bunch of dynamite. It didn't work out too well for them.

3.

Dear Whale. It was stupid of me to mention that other whale getting blown up with all the dynamite and everything. Totally insensitive. Sorry. I have *no grace*. I've been told this before. That I have no grace. I apologize. Just trying to make conversation. I'm no good at this. Sorry.

4.

Hey. Do you ever dress up as other animals? If so, what kind? It's almost Halloween out here. I was just wondering.

5.

Dear Whale: Halloween was totally lame. This one little kid came to the door dressed as a dolphin. But he had a net over him. And I said, *What's with the net?* And he said, *Every year hundreds of thousands of dolphins and whales are killed by the tuna fishing industry because they don't know how to avoid the nets.* And I thought he was insulting your intelligence, so I said: *Look motherfucker, you don't know a goddamn thing about whales. Get the fuck off my porch.*

6.

Maybe I overreacted there.

7.

Dear Whale: Do you ever see people swimming nearby and think to yourself, *I could really have some fun with this?*

8.

Like maybe you could surface right next to them and then yell something like, *Jonah! I've been looking for you!* And then open your mouth really wide?

9.

That's what I would do.

10.

I don't know—maybe whales have better things going on.

11.

Do whales believe in Providence?

12.

Do you ever float on your back and scrutinize the stars and see unexpected figures among them, like maybe shapes of other whales? Do you assign them names, and imagine stories for those make-believe creatures as they drift through the dark? Do those stories lend structure to your days and nights? Do they comfort the nervous waters, constellate the disjointed heavens, and render the marvelous in a manner that you can endure? Do you believe them?

13.

How cold is the bottom of the ocean? How crushing is the pressure down there?

14.

Do you ever worry that because your voice is impossible to hear, maybe no one will make the effort? That you can work really hard and try to be a good person and try to make a difference in your community, but then—at the end of the day—the waves will just swallow you whole? They will take you under. You'll disappear from the world. And you won't even leave a ripple on the surface.

Letter to Matthew Olzmann from a Flying Saucer

Listen son, when we shine this tractor beam on you,
you need to hold still. Not that stillness, son,
is something that can be *held*, but that's your language,
not ours. What we're saying, son,
is you keep skipping like a stone across a pond and we need

that to stop. What we're saying, son, is let the light
bring you home. Never mind the way
the tractor beam incinerates all it touches.
We're pretty certain this is safe. It's gonna work. Trust us.
There are things in your skull, son,

that do not belong to you, thoughts you can't explain,
songs you've never heard, colors you have no name for.
We're not saying you're special, son. We just needed a place
to store our luggage, and now we've got to extricate
that luggage and we need to extricate it all intact.

Think of the light as all the problems you need to face.
You're afraid of being alone in the world? You're afraid
that when the light shines on you, you're going
to be exposed and everyone will laugh? You're afraid
that you'll never be moderately competent? You need

to deal with that, son, and now is your big chance.
We're saying step into the light, son.
Never mind that you've doubted
whether or not the light is real. What is doubt, son?
You have a chance to be hauled into the sky.

Letter to Steve Orlen—

Orlen!! Just now, I was remembering
several winters back, when you were alive,
you were telling me that if you got stuck
while writing a poem, you'd try to make
a random seeming, radical move toward
a different subject, something to jar the work
onto newer terrain, and be sorted
out in later drafts. I like the idea of a *newer* terrain,
and I imagine you're there now—an explorer—abruptly
dropped into a curious landscape of stone and fallen trees.
You brush yourself off, look around, stroll toward
a summit near the horizon. Maybe you pick up
some rocks, examine them, and toss them aside.
Maybe your laugh startles the wildlife:
rabbits mostly, two or three gulls.
Is there any wind out there? I'm guessing you carry
a compass (which you ignore) and a flag (which you'll plant
at the island's highest point). There it is: a ridge that requires
only a day or two to ascend. There you look back
across an ocean, and glimpse the land you used to wander.
It's hard to see the link between here and there,
but that's what you were trying to teach: to connect
these disparate spaces. No separation: just vastness,
water, the smell of salt, islands yet to be discovered.

Phantom Route

One route starts near the horizon; another forms at the bottom
of Lake Erie. The route a phantom must follow might begin
in a graveyard. Another could wind along the length of a canyon.

One phantom carries a satchel full of fog, the next
pushes a cart of silence and bandages.

The houses where they arrive are usually abandoned,
sometimes demolished. Still, these couriers trudge onward.
They know what they're doing.

Look outside. What do you see?
A wine bottle bashed across the sidewalk?
A dog chasing a ball? Rain?

One phantom carries envelopes stuffed with whispers.
Another specializes in parcels filled
with ash, pencil shavings, bits of broken alarm clocks.

And who cares if the recipient is nameless,
or exists only in photographs? I've seen these figures
work, and they're the best in the business.

There are things I've wanted to say to you, times
when I had no words—Love,

I will be swept from this earth, erased—
and if I ever find a way,
these are the only messengers I'd trust:

a scrap of newspaper kicked up by the wind.
Taillights disappearing over the ridge.
A knock on the door when no one's home.

Letter to Jennifer Chang and Evan Rhodes Regarding a Variation in the Fabric of Time

...the concept of time has no meaning before the beginning of the universe. This was first pointed out by St. Augustine. When asked: "What did God do before he created the universe?" Augustine didn't reply: "He was preparing Hell for people who asked such questions."
   —*Stephen Hawking*

And who would ask St. Augustine such a question?
Perhaps Evan, but definitely Jen. Speaking of time,
on this date in history (back on April 1st, 1976),
the painter Max Ernst died. Tomorrow,
marks the anniversary of his birth (April 2nd, 1891).
Do you like his paintings? Wait,

first, let me say something about highways.
Driving through the mountains in a thunderstorm
is not my favorite pastime, but sometimes it needs
to be done—like when I need to get to Michigan—
and I hate it the whole way
and my nerves turn to tension wires
and the journey blurs from mountains to more mountains
to ridges and valleys and switchbacks and hills,
then smaller hills, and then—

then there's Ohio!
Where the roads are flat the way God intended them to be!
Where the highway on the GPS is a straight line!
And it remains a straight line for the next forever or so!

I'd celebrate this state and its majestic flatness,
but something odd happens 181 miles in.
There's the exit that I would've taken to visit you
if it was last year again,
and if you still lived there,
and if I was going to visit you.

What did God do before the invention of the American Midwest?
Now it's just another exit, and I think it's strange
how a place goes from being a destination
to just another landmark I blow by at 70 miles-per-hour,
and I wonder if Ohio has any idea how much less it has
without you two in it. I'm talking about the problem of time.
Which brings us to Max Ernst.

He died on April 1st, and was born on April 2nd.
I like the way the anniversary of the beginning comes after
the anniversary of the end.

Francis Bacon says, *Time seemeth to be of the nature of a river
or stream, which carrieth down to us that which is light and blown up,
and sinketh and drowneth that which is weighty and solid.*

Fairly often, I too have sinketh and drowneth
in the River of Time! I too have been unable
to distinguish the past from the future.
It's like being in Michigan now, where I don't live,
but still have an apartment,
because I thought I'd be back much sooner than this.

Have you ever heard that saying: *You can never go home again?*
If a man can be born the day after he dies,
maybe it's possible that we never really leave.

Your house still exists back there in Bowling Green.
In fact, they've rented it to a fraternity.
There's a gaggle of shirtless dudes on the front lawn,
a small garden of flattened Miller Lite cans
where all the flowers used to grow.

Letter to My Future Neighbors

Because this is New Hampshire,
there's a 97% chance you are not Black.
My wife insists that I tell you that she is
(she would like this known *before* you meet her).

She wants me to mention it will be safer for her this way,
safer than if she were to ring your doorbell
and introduce herself, by herself.

Not that she's worried that you've got a shotgun
and will shoot her through the door, but
she does want me to point out that this
is a thing that "accidentally" happens these days.

She just doesn't want anyone to get suspicious
when she parks her own car in front of her own house,
or when she carries groceries (which she did not steal)
to the door of her own house.

Not that you would do that, of course.
You're going to love her.
Her name is Vievee and you'll find her very approachable.

The other day, I looked out the window of the apartment
where we currently live, and in the parking lot
she was chatting with a couple who moved in nearby.

I was happy because she looked happy
and she was pointing to our place, as if to invite
them over, saying: *Hi. Yes, it's wonderful*

to meet you. *Yes, I live in that unit right there.*
That one. Right there. No, I live here. No, I said,
I live here. These are my keys. This is my car.

No, I'm saying that I live here. Not visiting,
I live here. No, I live here.

Letter to a Man Drowning in a Folktale

Sometimes my friend and I would race home from school,
to sit on the floor of his living room,
at the feet of his grandfather who would demolish us
with fables and myths he'd carried
since the world was younger. Full of danger
and heroes, each

was designed to teach ethics or wreck us
with confusion. *Choices and consequences!*
he would say. Like the tale about the boy
who saves a man from drowning,
and that man becomes a general who later
obliterates that boy's village in some future war.

These stories contradicted the well-tested codes of morality
that we, as nine-year-olds, knew to be accurate:
Saving lives is good, destroying villages is bad,
and never shall these two paths intersect.

I'm older now, less patient with fables.
The lines of demarcation between decent
and deranged are distinct.
Like these forms on my desk about organ donation:
the how, where, when, and why.

It seems like a good, practical thing. The world
spreads out in neat little rows; the map makes sense.

Until my friend Dave calls. Dave, with his Dave-ish wisdom

saying, *What if. What if. What if*
your heart goes to a Nazi or a serial killer or something?

Like all great thinkers, he is prone to abstraction,
hypotheticals unmoored from reality. And yet,
last week a white wave of anger rolled across my TV screen,
a mob of Tiki Torches and Hitler salutes.

So maybe Dave's not that far off.
Is humanity good or bad? Today, it feels like a coin flip.

                              Meanwhile you—
a hypothetical man drowning in a folktale—
you are out there in my future.
Sinking in an ocean or waiting on an operating table.

Maybe you're a hydrologist and have devoted your life
to making clean drinking water accessible for everyone.
Or maybe you build electric chairs.

See? Dave is kind of right: I have no idea
who you really are. What does it mean?

It means you could be the doomed man among the waves,
the ocean could be your fate,
and the disconnected heart I lob toward it
could be the life buoy that keeps you afloat.

Or I could be the ocean,
and the heart I keep to myself is the drowning man.
Or you are the life buoy, and your continued
breathing is my only chance at redemption.

There are moments when compassion is a yes
or no question. We can donate our organs
to strangers or be buried with all our worldly possessions.
We can save the drowning man, or just think about it.

Sometimes there can be no hesitation.

And then I hesitate.

Letter to a Canyon

I saw your emptiness, and believed

you were the absence
of the stone
landscape from which you'd been cut.

But the stone, extending to the horizon,
said, *No.* The inverse was true: you,
in your emptiness, were not the absence

of the stone: the stone
was actually the absence of the emptiness.

I make a terrible emptiness.
Even when I try for emptiness,
I fill everything with accidents.

Last week, I got pulled over for going
twenty-five miles-per-hour over the speed limit
I didn't even notice how fast the mountains were moving.
My wife said, *You could've died doing that.*

Just once, I want to be moderately competent,
able to pay attention long enough to notice I'm here.
To focus well enough to not drive off a cliff.

Years ago, I took a meditation class.
The teacher lit candles and played
The Gentle Sound of Wind or *The Soothing
Mystery of Rain* on a tape deck.

You are relaxed, she said.
Feel the light coursing through your arms, she said.

I never made it to the end of a class awake.

She said, *Feel the empty vessel filling with light*,
but already I'd filled the empty vessel with the steady
darkness of dreaming.

What does a canyon dream?
Did you know it's impossible to tell time in a dream?
Like you, I too was skeptical of this,
but in a dream,
clocks don't work correctly (if their hands move at all).

What is time to a canyon?
I dreamed of water woven
through me, though water takes everything apart.
It's how we are born, but also
how the rocks that make the canyon are turned

into smaller rocks, then pebbles,
then carried out to sea:
everyone we know, everyone we've been.

THREE

Letter to Matthew Olzmann from the Roman Empire

Two or three mornings per week, I wake up, and say, Dang,
I'm the Roman Empire! I'm the Land where Jupiter swings
his mighty marble columns! Check out these temples!
Check out these fine-ass aqueducts! I've got the Arch of Janus,
the Arch of Titus, and the Arch of Septimius Severus.
What does one do with so many Arches? Beats me,
but two or three mornings per week, I wake up, ready
to conquer, ready to ride my chariot down the block again.
Look at these golden rims. Look at this platinum sideboard.
Gaze upon this diamond-encrusted crossbar and yoke.

The rest of the week, I just want to stay inside. I just want
to read a book and go to bed. This happens, I reckon,
to everyone. You might not understand now, but you will.

Initially, you'll enter the world with a cry that soars like
a bald eagle. The audience will applaud your first steps.
You'll go to school and solve the conundrum of two plus two.
You'll discover who Marcus Aurelius is. Or was.
You'll get a job, smile for the cameras, subjugate
a couple of promising territories. It'll be one victory lap
after another, but before you know it—Visigoths

scrabble the horizon and your garage needs a new roof.
You press on, govern admirably, mow the lawn. But
your legions quibble and caterwaul, your boss calls
on the weekends, and some new god begins a campaign
of turning water into wine in the neighbor's yard.

Suddenly, you can't remember where you put your keys.
Next, your praetors have all been corrupted. Pillars
crack, molder. No one's been near the Colosseum in years.

Letter to the Connecticut River Monster

I want to tell you about a body they pulled
from the river. But to tell you, I have to find you.
And when I search for you, the first place I go
is not the rocks at the water's edge,
not the mud-streaked and alluvial lowlands,
nor the clearing among the reeds
where the river widens; instead, I begin
wading through the blue
screen of my computer, and even there,
you're impossible to locate.
Few pictures. Few witness accounts.
You don't even have a flashy nickname.
I applaud you for keeping a low profile online.
There's something religious about the recluse.
When we imagine the lives of saints,
each is always desolate, a solitary figure
beyond the fires of the encampment.
In the dark, past the perimeters of civilization,
there's a terror in being
unknown and unknowable. In the waters
of the internet, all the animals are faster
and more self-righteous than you. It's never
like the movies where the fin circles before
the teeth are shown. Instead, they glide beneath
the surface, anonymous and clean.
Maybe you choose to hide in the river forever,
the way a man might choose to hide forever
in so many sleeping pills, the lights all going out
one by one along the shoreline. When I walk down

to this river at night, there's no one wading into it.
No one about to jump from the bridge that crosses
the river, bridging this state and the next.
It's just me. In the half-light: the shape of a doe
lowers her head like a ladle to the Lethe.
In the old myths, that river would cause
one to forget everything that ever was.
The river keeps on with its insistent murmuring.
You are nowhere to be found.

The Dead Letter Office

Envelopes, mystery packages, boxes without postage
and sealed with three different kinds of tape: The Wheel

of the Mail continues to roll.
No matter what you've heard, here's how it works.

No expense is spared.
Satellite surveillance, bloodhounds, witch doctors:

we'll use anything to find
the ones who must be found, deliver

all that must be delivered.
Even if they say it can't be delivered

because you—genius, you—wrote a letter
to Perseus of Ancient Greece,

to [name illegible] at 366 [street illegible],
to Mary, Mother of God;

the address was incorrect, nonexistent, located in space.
Matters not. We'll find those

who must be found and give them what must be given.
Unless the things they must be given

can't be delivered, in which case they'll be returned.
Unless they can't be returned, in which case they'll be destroyed.

Unless they can't be destroyed (i.e. they contain objects of value),
in which case they'll be sold at auction.

Unless the objects of value include weapons,
narcotics, or pornography, in which case

they will be neither sold nor destroyed.

Letter to a Man Who, within a Year of Being Struck by Lightning, Had Previously Been Hit by a Cement Truck and Bitten by a Tarantula

My friends and I are having a debate. They think
you're cursed, the unluckiest man in the world.
Ordinarily, I'd agree. However,
because I'm told I need to change my "negative" outlook,
I "choose" to think of you as blessed.
After all, you lived. Let's say, you've been gifted
with abilities, like those bestowed by secret
government laboratories or gamma rays. Gifted,
and if you were to enroot this gift,
you could expand the CV to include titles such as:
The man who was digested in the stomach of a tornado
and lived. Who kissed the volcano wet on the mouth
and lived. Who sung into the maelstrom, then found
his life flourishing, boundless and full.
Where Ayo and Jami tell me they see a *harbinger of doom*,
I see *just a coincidence* or *what a fantastic opportunity!*
The man who mourned the loss of his uncles
or parents or sisters and brothers and lived.
Who felt abandoned by Providence and lived.
Who reached for his dreams and found
them like gypsum sand through his fingers.
Whose fingers were like sausages struck by a mallet.
My pals, sitting across from me, use words like *catastrophe*.
But I, with my improved attitude, now have
the agility of mind to say, *Could've been worse!*
A housing crisis. Hunger. A tremor of fascism
in the foundation of the place you call home.

I'm doing very good at optimism!
I'm saying that I believe in *you*, which means
I'm trying to believe in the spirit of humanity.
The spirit of one who sat across from Death and lived.
Who played chess with Azrael and lived.
What is luck anyway? A black cat?
A full moon? A walk beneath a ladder?
Stop me please while I yawn from boredom.
A bolt of lightning, a cement truck, an itsy-bitsy spider bite?
Just a passing trepidation. Not dread.
Not terror. Just a brief sense of disquiet,
whose sails pass soundlessly through the harbors
of our lives, while you and I stand
radiant on the shore. The trees are on fire.
The armies have already gathered.
Someone is building a golf course.

Letter to Jamaal May Regarding the Existence of Unicorns

I thought of home, and how you were telling me
that when you tell people there are birds in Detroit,
they think it's a metaphor.

This happens to me too, except instead of birds,
I usually tell them there are unicorns,
and instead thinking it's a metaphor,
they think I'm lying to them.

They think this because

    A) I am, and
    B) Well I thought I had another reason,
        but I guess it's mostly just reason A.

What they don't realize is there actually *was* a unicorn once.
But only one. (Not plural like I tell them).

A boy begged his parents to get him a horse.
They gave in but screwed up.
Instead, he got a quivering thing
with a whinny and a white horn. At school,
it was chaos and anger on show-and-tell day:
What's wrong with your ugly horse, his classmates sneered.

Their parents called his parents to rail against
the troublemaker, the kid who wouldn't *play by the rules.*

Jamaal, let me tell you, I have little patience
for these people and their utter paucity of imagination.

Anyway, week after week, a mob of small tyrants
traipsed by that kid's house to terrorize the horse.
They'd spit, they'd point,
They'd bare their stupid, stupid, little teeth.

It was more than any kid could take, and torn
between his love of the horse and his desire
not to be different, the boy crumbled the way
all things crumble when they're kicked
by the blunt and uninspired.
He snuck out one night with a plan in his brain
and his father's hacksaw in his backpack.
It was the wrong move and the next morning,
the thing was dead. Discovering the body, he wept
and wept, rushed to recover the horn but already—
it was powder, pale as ash, coarse as sea salt.

As for the kid with the dead horse?
Imagine the next day at school. How would he respond?
Tears? A damming finger pointed
in the direction of his classmates? Perhaps he pretended
not to even see them; he simply walked right by:
an exile leaving home forever.

Behind him, if one cared to look,
we might have seen most
of the known world: zealous currents, ravaged pastures,
skies that shudder as if trampled by hooves.

Letter to Larry Levis

As if by some unholy, digital sorcery, last week,
when I typed your last name into the internet,
my computer came back with,
Did you mean to type Levi's®? And I said,
No, I meant Larry Levis. And my computer said,
Did you mean to type Larry Levi's®? And I said,
Lord, grant me the mercy to bring no hammer
down through thy machine. And my computer said,
All Levi's Brand Apparel, on sale at select locations!
And I said, *I give up.* This must be
your more famous ancestor
who made clothing from bolts of the cloth called *denim.*

In the early days, it was overalls
and was popular among miners and farmers.
Later, it was jeans and jackets and revered among
all who were alive. These new garments were praised
for their durability, meaning: they could last.
What *lasts* anymore, Larry? Some of your poems,
I hope, but not the cities, rivers, or roads we chart
from one end of the imagination to the other.
And never our names. Yours, for example,
expunged and replaced as I type it.
Even the clothing sold to me by Levi's
wears thin, has holes.
The left knee. The right pocket,
where I keep spare change. Everything falls through.
I get up. I walk away from the desk.
In your name, I leave
this trail of coins.

Letter to Matthew Olzmann from Ross White, Re: The Tardigrade

Dehydrate the water bear
        and desiccation fractures his DNA.
                He'll be all right for the next ten years.

Moisten the little beast
        just a little drop, and his metabolism
                reacts like a long-dormant volcano erupting,

cells molting like magma
        to allow in large molecules,
                foreign genetic material cooling into place.

He's practically alien
        to himself in a few dry generations,
                part plant, part fungus, part bacteria,

a kind of genetic recyclery,
        patchwork quilt of organism,
                blast furnace, melting pot, crucible,

symphony of the mestizo,
        cognate across the same body.
                He is not a thing of elegance, wobbly

and occasionally swept up
        by currents oceanic and morphological,
                molting at inappropriate moments,

playful in hot springs
     and sediment, reticent
          under layers of solid ice.

Who wants to be made
     of just one thing? Friend, I graft
you to me with such gratitude.

Letter to Matthew Olzmann, Sent Telepathically from a Flock of Pigeons While Surrounding Him on a Park Bench in Detroit, Michigan

You're not going to share that, are you?
You're just going to eat that entire sandwich all by yourself, aren't you?

Well, congratulations on your new sandwich.
A fine purchase, Olzmann. Eating is important. Coincidentally,

we'd like to discuss one of today's most critical social issues: food security.
We want a simple conversation about sustainability, malnutrition and fair trade.

Quit telling us to go away.
You're talking to pigeons, for Christ's sake.

Someone might see you.
Someone might think you think we're listening to you.

We're not listening. We're *watching*.
Go ahead and tell someone that. Say: *The pigeons are watching me.*

See how that works out. We just want to talk
about pesticides, deforestation, and widespread famine.

Let's chat about climate change, and wars where hunger
is used as a weapon, and how ten million tons
of uneaten crops are destroyed each year.

How's that sandwich? It's a BLT? Really? Does the bacon
taste like factory farms where animals are castrated

without painkillers, then live their lives in sweltering cages,
in their own shit, unable even to turn around?

Just wondering. Looks tasty.
You should drop a little bit on the ground for your friends down here.

No, we won't *just go away*. What would that say about us
if we remained silent. What does it say about you

that you just want to eat your lunch and look
at the trees, and say things like, *What a marvelous day!*

We think you're underestimating us.

Behind our backs you probably call us *rats of the air*,
flying rats, or *rats with wings*.

You think we're clumsy and unrefined.
But we're the most sophisticated beings to ever wobble across the sky.

Your scientists are obsessed with us.
In their laboratories, we've shown a fundamental
understanding of the nature of time.

We can distinguish between cubism and impressionism.
We can recognize written languages,
guide lost sailors to shore, and diagnose cancers.

Because of our excellent sense of direction
we've taken flight with little notes attached to us.
We've done this for armies, emperors, post offices, and smugglers.

For centuries, we've carried your words over mountain ranges,
farmlands, corn fields, wheat fields,
lakes, orchards, plateaus, rivers
and the rivers you poisoned, forests
and the forests you leveled,

the cities you built,
and the ruins of the cities you built.

Wing Case

A case extension added to a main letter or flats distribution case or to a
main carrier case that protrudes at an angle on either side of the main case.
—*United States Postal Service, "Glossary of Postal Terms"*

Or, let's say, a case for actual wings. A seraph?
One weary seraph, malfunctioning and tired

from the long fight against gravity and malevolence.
His wings. They're removable. Designed to be

unloosed when the burden of flight exceeds
the desire for flight, when one begins to plummet,

or can no longer bear being this alone this far
above the city. He lays the wings in the wing case

the way a musician lays down his guitar, when he knows
its last note has been played and the music is no longer

inside him. It's true: music resides in the body,
not the instrument, and it's possible for the body

to tire, to breathe out for the last time. So the wings
go in the case, and the case is returned to the factory.

Meanwhile, the body becomes a body again. It might
stroll through the city a few more times, or it might

power down for the evening, call it a night.
And the wings in their case? At the factory,

they inspect the wings for damage.
Some are ravaged beyond repair.

Others are coated in oil, tears, and tar. But a few
are so clean, their feathers so soft and complicated,

one can hardly believe they could have
carried someone, anyone, all the way here.

Letter to the Person Who Carved His Initials into the Oldest Living Longleaf Pine in North America

—Southern Pines, NC

Tell me what it's like to live without
curiosity, without awe. To sail
on clear water, rolling your eyes
at the kelp reefs swaying
beneath you, ignoring the flicker
of mermaid scales in the mist,
looking at the world and feeling
only boredom. To stand
on the precipice of some wild valley,
the eagles circling, a herd of caribou
booming below, and to yawn
with indifference. To discover
something primordial and holy.
To have the smell of the earth
welcome you to everywhere.
To take it all in and then,
to reach for your knife.

Letter to Matthew Olzmann from a Traffic Light in Durham, North Carolina

Actually, I'm less of a traffic cop, more
of an amateur thaumaturgist. What miracles might
I perform, you ask? I adjure the passage of time.
Wait here, I say. *Go ahead,* I say. And in fits,

your world stops. Then starts. Then stops.
Then proceeds. Then ceases. Then ensues.
Then halts. Then pulses and lurches forward,
like blood through a valve to storm

the command center in your cranium. Up there,
something seethes at every red light, authorizes
your clenched teeth, your mad muttering of, *God,
please make this light turn green.* And I say,

Nope. And I say, *Not yet.* And I say, *Remain
in place and observe.* Look: there goes your world.
And there it goes again. How is it that you
who have begged to believe in anything, see only

this one road before you? This one delay. This brief
intermission. Not the wonderment of highways
it touches. Not the intersections I present, void
of collisions, all windblown and ghost-town quiet.

Not the order I foist upon each crossroad
you encounter. These zippy motorcycles.
These sleek sedans. None of them broadsiding you.
No fiery ruin. No Wreck-of-Matthew.

Each vessel, with a particular terminus, and each vessel,
I send on its way.

FOUR

Constellation Route

I spent at least five minutes looking for my glasses
when they were on my head.

I wish this were a parable about how everything we search for
is closer than we expect, but we all know
it's an allegory about futility,

and how, in the Garden,
Adam was given just one simple directive
and look how that turned out.

Already, I can hear the voices saying, *You're being
hyperbolic and overdramatic.* But those are the voices
of people who can find things
when they are wearing those things,
people who don't leave

their car windows open overnight in the rain,
who don't push when the door says pull,
who don't trip over their own feet
then spring back up hoping no one saw.

I've spent many hours hoping no one saw
each monumental effort, each inevitable fall.

In moments like these, I want to believe
in a cosmic plan, a higher power orchestrating it all,
that every blunder has a reason built inside it.

The Terracotta Army and penicillin were discovered
by accident. Same with nuclear fusion
and the inventions of rubber and the microwave oven.

I am good at accidents.
Less good at finding meaning in them.

A *star route* is an obsolete postal term
for a route given to an outside contractor instead
of a regular mail carrier. Records identified this route
with an asterisk, a star, hence its name,
though I prefer to imagine an alternate etymology:

another timeline, a couple hundred years ago,
a messenger, on horseback, races to the end.
Let's say, he gets wildly lost. It's night.
Lonely. He glances to the sky—

it looks like chaos, a tangle of lights resisting
all interpretation. Then, inside that disorder,
he finds one light that makes sense, and that's enough

to guide him to the next stop. I too, look at the world
trying to find the one thing that makes sense.
Let's say there are many of us doing this.

Each following a different lodestar through
our confusions. Calamities. Self-inflicted catastrophes.

The pacemaker and x-ray were lucky mistakes.
Radio waves emitted by planets and the sound
of the Big Bang—all found via fortuitous errors.

Tell me that's not random; these suggest
a connection among incongruent paths,
recognizable shapes made by disparate points of light.

Not an individual star route but a constellation.
The Rosetta Stone, also discovered by accident,
unlocked the secrets to understanding hieroglyphics.

The shards of the vase I just knocked over:
less mysterious, equally urgent to translate.

I want those pieces to be a message, a divine code, a map
back to Asgard, Eden, or Detroit. In my hands,
they appear to be random pieces of clay.

I rifle through all the kitchen drawers.
I search for the glue.

Return to Sender

To the topsoil and subsoil: returned.
To humus and blistered rock: returned.

To the kingdom of the masked chafer beetle,
the nematode and the root maggot: returned.

To the darkness where a solitary star-nosed mole
arranges her possessions and pulses

through a slow hallway, and to the vastness
where twenty thousand garden ants compose

a tangled metropolis: returned.
It was summer, and they lowered

a body into the ground. I did not say
they lowered you into the ground.

It seemed like you were elsewhere, but the preacher
insisted: *And now, he returns to the one who made him.*

Most likely, he meant: God. But I thought
he meant the earth, that immensity

where everything changes, buzzes, is alive again and—
Amen.

Letter to My Car's Radiator

Like a bull, the transmission fluid boils and charges
through its arena of tubes toward you,
and like a matador, you make all of it miss you completely.
Look: it's on the highway a quarter mile behind us!

Congratulations! I'm impressed by your artistry.
But if you could kindly knock that shit off,
I'd be truly grateful.

A man stands next to his broken vehicle
on a dirt road in the American South. The sky
grows dark. The forest, even darker.
And those low sounds from the trees
and the gurgling creek—sounds that sound like murder—
could be the mud-filled groans of the Carolina gopher frog.
Or, the early hunger pangs of a zombie apocalypse.
No way to tell. Dan McKernan (friend of the author,
amateur zombie expert) says the first thing to do
is search your car for a zombie-killing instrument,
anything available, most likely: a tire iron or crowbar.

I cannot confirm or deny whether the protagonist
of this story crouched by the side of his car,
a tire iron in his fist, fear in his eyes,
and Armageddon in his heart.

I cannot verify that—around him in the dark—twigs
snapped like small bones, and dry leaves shuffled
like ankles of the dead inching closer.

The point is: I feel helpless.
The point is: the world is going to devour us, and both

the thing-made-by-man
(i.e. the car and its system of tubes and coils that
spit steam into the gravel and sky)

and the thing-made-by-nature
(i.e. the forest, the darkness, the frogs,
the zombies, and so forth)

are beyond my ability to comprehend, repair, or control.
Does this sound ridiculous? Absurd?
Let me remind you: I'm writing a letter
to a radiator of a 2006 Dodge Neon.
The Absurd is the only country I've known.
I've been mapping its territory since I learned to hold a crayon.
And you, Dear Radiator, have been of little assistance
in my negotiations with this topography.

One of the earliest attempts to map the known world
comes from Babylon. It's damaged, but the labels
of at least three distinct islands can be understood.

One where the sun rises.
One where the sun is hidden.
One beyond the wings of any bird.

We all travel toward that last island, and when
it gets this dark out here, Earth is ancient again.
Tonight, everything that flutters up beyond that tree line
is impossible to see.

Letter to Matthew Olzmann from Mike Scalise
Concerning Love and Echoes

Dear Olzmann—

Loren and I have been dressing the same lately. It's an accident we fail, regularly, to avoid. We find, before leaving the house, as though waking from a trance, that we're both wearing jeans and gray sweatshirts, or black shirts and brown pants, or blue shirts and gray pants.

We try sometimes to preempt it. *I'll be wearing black tonight,* she will say. *I'll be in plaid,* I will say. But most times we forget, which triggers this inane litigation we pretend to dislike; an intimate, meaningless vaudeville. Who is dressing like who, who will yield.

I've been thinking a lot about this impulse we have, to—what, exactly? Mimic? Echo?

Influence mirroring is the concept for it on the Internet, and it's pitched as a horrible feat of dissolved ego. *Coupling is to relent,* the wisdom seems to go.

There's an old amusement park by the house I grew up in outside of Pittsburgh, a pocket of clacking rides along a riverbank of dead steel mill carcasses, curled in arthritic rust. Whole families dress in the same white pants or gold shirts or hats or denim to go to the park on summer days. They ride roller coasters *as one.* They eat corn dogs *as one.*

I used to think it was punishment to be so oblivious. I admired the regality of aloneness.

Now I'm married almost fifteen years and know someone so well I don't even know how well I know them. Loren and I discover, when we try to leave the house, that we still bind to one another even while we don't try. Our feet touch while we sleep.

Maybe we are operating beyond ourselves in that way.

Maybe we're at work on a project, while unawake, that neither of us can truly see.

Because, Olz—those mills along the riverbank died, but that amusement park survives. The denim families going there for corn dogs survive, too. What if we have to be a little bit unconscious to do that work for so long?

And what if that work requires a uniform?

Daylight Container

Mail transported at a specified transportation rate in containers
(owned by carriers) on airline flights scheduled to depart between
6:01 a.m. and 8:59 p.m.
—*United States Postal Service, "Glossary of Postal Terms"*

Do not place other types of light in the Daylight Container.
Not the blue light of the TV that glows like loneliness
into living room after living room across the country.
Not the illuminated billboards as they promise
a Jaguar and lottery tickets. Only daylight.

Not the strings of Christmas bulbs your neighbor leaves
up through July. Not the bonfires on the horizon
or the moon that puckers like a poisoned apple. Only daylight.

Only light that flits through clouds, circles you
and trembles like a hummingbird. Only light
from the sun gathered in preapproved Ball jars,
insulated coolers, or padded envelopes.

Did you think this was elusive, holy, impossible
to contain? Maybe it is.

But if you manage to capture some, you can take it
to a Daylight Container to be saved for later usage,
or sent to anyone you love. But only between
the hours of 6:01 a.m. and 8:59 p.m. Send it too early,
the light will falter forward, wheeze, and collapse.
And if you send it too late? Then it's just too late.

Letter to a Younger Version of Myself Who Had Never Known Hunger

Everyone here loves someone. *My father*
is sick; I'm picking up some things for him,
one might say. *Three kids. Trying to get us back*
on our feet, another tells you.

Everyone here loves someone and because
they love someone: Four cans of corn.
Three bags of rice. Two boxes of cereal.

They took the bus after work.
They walked from two towns over.
A bag of flour. Fresh produce.
One pound of frozen chicken.
Because the company downsized.
Because an unexpected illness.
Because the insurance agency had no answers
for what was damaged in the night.

In the Offices of Yearning, Hunger has no interest
in hearing how forty percent of the food
we produce will go unsold, uneaten, discarded.
It doesn't care if you've gone to college
or have a blood clot in your arm.
It offers no discounts when someone breaks
into your home and sets fire to the kitchen.
If you made a bad investment.
If you were in an accident.
If you stole a couple credit cards, got arrested,
and now, no one in this town will hire you.

One day, you'll find your way here.
Because everyone here loves someone,
and by then, you will to.
You haven't met her yet, but there will be a day
when you'll be hungry, and she will feed you.

I still remember the care she took with each meal,
and though I didn't know it then,
the food we enjoyed came from a place like this.
Everyone here loves someone
and the person she loved was me.
Perhaps I asked for more
when there wasn't any left to give,
and only then did I understand.

When you arrive at that juncture,
you'll feel a bridge collapse inside you.
That feeling will be shame but also love,
and years later you might find yourself here
unloading a truck, sweeping the floor,
wearing a name tag and sorting tomatoes.
Where is this place that I'm telling you about?
It doesn't matter. It could be anywhere.

You're holding a carton of eggs.
You're holding a bottle of milk.
You're holding the unspoken history
of each kindness you have received
though have not always felt you deserved.

And now it's just a single loaf of bread.
That's what you hold. And you are here

to place that offering
in someone else's hands.

Some Notes from Vievee on the Kindness of Shepherds

1.

Sweet sheep
 wayward and willing
look down over the bridge again
wander halfway up
 the mountain again
one loses herself in the limbs again

A shepherd combs the forest
A shepherd combs the burrs from the wool

2.

Into the creek that one wades again
 follows it to the mouth
of the river   Into the river he swims to get her
And the days grow so long and hot

He lays her on the moss

3.

 She jumps through the clover
cool and darkly green before the bloom

 He finds her
 He always finds her
Before the bees can sting
 After the wasps have stung

Sometimes honey-drunk by the side of a pool
 table

Howling along with some wolf
No good sheep
would make that sound

4.

The shepherd whispers
lamb-love
bad-baby
there's nothing to forgive

5.

He strokes her head again
She falls asleep in his arms again
        then slips away early
runs toward the ledge again
        All night some wolf howls
                At midnight the coyote's
fickle interest   unkempt charm
        She's having a bourbon
        She's singing some sorrow-song

The shepherd picks her up and takes her home
Wiley sheep
                Woolen cross to bear

6.

Once he found her in the doorway
                        half-dead
He made a pillow of himself
Let her sleep
        In this way she stopped having nightmares
He warmed her with his own bare body
        In this way she forgets the unbearable

Explains
     A wolf knows no mercy
     A coyote knows less
Tells her
     They live to bite
          and tell
Gives her
     a secret name so delightful—

7.
This is my story to tell my way

8.
She had measured her weight against the beams
She swallowed half the medicine cabinet

How to understand the shepherd's kindness
when some nights the moon leaves
     a trail of light she follows to
     a man at the bar smiling as if kind

Those nights the shepherd puts an arm like a crook
     around her waist
     and brings her back

     Who else will dress her wounds and
          never blame her
    for her

whom he knows to be more lamb than not
     more his than ever

Letter to Someone Living Fifty Years from Now

Most likely, you think we hated the elephant,
the golden toad, the thylacine and all variations
of whale harpooned or hacked into extinction.

It must seem like we sought to leave you nothing
but benzene, mercury, the stomachs
of sea gulls rippled with jet fuel and plastic.

You probably doubt that we were capable of joy,
but I assure you we were.

We still had the night sky back then,
and like our ancestors, we admired
its illuminated doodles
of scorpion outlines and upside-down ladles.

Absolutely, there were some forests left!
Absolutely, we still had some lakes!

I'm saying, it wasn't all lead paint and sulfur dioxide.
There were bees back then, and they pollinated
a euphoria of flowers so we might
contemplate the great mysteries and finally ask,
Hey guys, what's transcendence?

And then all the bees were dead.

An Offering

I made a miniature fire,
and I'll send it to you if you think it will help.

It's small: just twigs, just dry leaves,
just hopes and scattered wishes, but it's a fire,
and I'll send it to you if you need a little fire.

It's a fire and you can have it if you'd like it,
if you could use such a thing, a burning thing,
though, admittedly, not an especially luminous burning thing,
but still—a miniature fire.

Prometheus stole fire from Olympus and was manacled
to a mountain. In Rome, Vulcan could only be worshipped
outside the city. This was to protect the citizens
from his ashes: falling everywhere, searing everything.
In Eden, after Man was banished from the Garden,
an angel with a sword of fire was sent to guard the grounds.

And there's fire again, in the center of the crowd
demanding liberty. And there's fire again, with a fistful
of daisies, singing *I love you, I love you* and leading a revolt.

This is not that kind of fire. It's a humble fire: quiet,
peculiar, and forgiving of others. Not destined to be coveted
by gods or thieves. But I swear I'll put it in a cast-iron pot
or maybe a mason jar and set it on your doorstep
or present it to you in person if you'd like a modest fire.

It won't bring back the dead, assuage your nightmares,
or ameliorate a widening rift in our earth.
It's only a small fire. Shy, uncertain,
and a little aloof. It might warm your hands.
It might cast a brief light in this duplicitous dark.

Though I can't guarantee even that.
It's only a miniature fire. But I made it for you
and if you want it, it's yours.

Conversion

A change in an employee's status or tenure from one category of employment to another, such as from part-time to full-time or from noncareer to career.

—*United States Postal Service, "Glossary of Postal Terms"*

The cell divides and a hundred million years later,
it's a bull shark or Sophocles. Not sure which;
not sure how these things work. Point is:
things change, evolve, move forward.

You get the job, get promoted, get fired.
Lead becomes gold, then one day it doesn't.
The sun orbits the earth, then one day it doesn't.
The whale gets legs, gets bored with land, goes back

to the ocean, the legs are now a metaphor. Nothing
certain, nothing written in stone that can't be unwritten
by the hammer. The world keeps trying to end itself
because it wants to end, then one day it doesn't.

You get homesick. Get heartburn. Get a strange yearning
to pray when looking at photographs or cell phone towers.
You have a hard time adjusting to your new status,
station, or impending fate. You believed one thing,

now you believe something else. The earth has ice caps,
then one day it doesn't. Everything: converted
to a newer thing. Meanwhile: old gods become lesser gods,
become priests leaving offerings on someone else's altar.

The god of war grows up to sell pocketknives at a pawn shop.
The goddess of carrots peddles sinus medications.
The messenger god now brings your mail—
and there he is, right on schedule, one house to the next.

This always stuns me: the way an envelope arrives; how we
still reach toward one another, how this correspondence
endures: one figure approaches your door with a satchel
full of sand, pigeon feathers, sorrows, and names.

NOTES

All definitions of postal terminology, including those used incorrectly in these poems, are taken from "Publication 32—Glossary of Postal Terms" by the United States Postal Service and were accessed online: https://about.usps.com/publications/pub32.pdf

This book's first epigraph is a paraphrased translation from Herodotus and inscribed across the front of the James A. Farley Post Office in New York City.

The poem "While Sleeping" by Wisława Szymborska, excerpted as the second epigraph for this book, can be found in her collection *Map: Collected and Last Poems*, translated by Clare Cavanagh and Stanisław Barańczak.

"Letter to Bruce Wayne" borrows an idea from the short story "Book of Sand" by Jorge Luis Borges. In that story, the narrator says, "I remember having read that the best place to hide a leaf is in a forest" and then hides a book in the Argentine National Library. It's unclear where Borges/the narrator of that story previously read that (possibly nowhere as it's a work of fiction) but he could have been referring to G.K. Chesterton's "Father

Brown" mysteries in which one character asks, "Where does a wise man hide a leaf?" and another responds, "In a forest." But he also could have been referring to anyone who has suggested the idea of hiding something in plain sight.

William Shatner's words in "Letter to William Shatner" are from my memory of a recorded Priceline.com message. I'll note that Kingda Ka is no longer the world's fastest roller coaster. It's possible that he actually said it's the world's "tallest" roller coaster (which is still true in 2021). Also, it's possible that the recording was made before 2010 when Kingda Ka would've actually been the fastest roller coaster. If there is any factual error in the poem, dear reader, I assure you the mistake was made by my memory. No mistakes were made by William Shatner who, I'm confident, fact-checked everything and did not make mistakes.

The italicized lines at the beginning of "Letter Beginning with Two Lines by Czesław Miłosz" are from Miłosz's poem "Dedication" (translated by Czesław Miłosz).

Steve Orlen's words in "Letter to Steve Orlen" are from an email sent by Steve Orlen and received by the author on February 14, 2007.

The quote used as an epigraph for "Letter to Jennifer Chang and Evan Rhodes Regarding a Variation in the Fabric of Time" is from Stephen Hawking's *A Brief History of Time*. The Francis Bacon quote used in the same poem was found on the internet and is probably wrong.

The opening stanza of "Letter to Jamaal May Regarding the Existence of Unicorns" refers to and paraphrases part of Jamaal's poem "There Are Birds Here." A response from Jamaal May to "Letter to Jamaal May Regarding the Existence of Unicorns" can be found in his collection *The Big Book of Exit Strategies*.

The tree referenced in "Letter to the Oldest Living Longleaf Pine in North America" and later in "Letter to the Person Who Carved His Initials into the Oldest Living Longleaf Pine in North America" can be found on the grounds of the Weymouth Woods Sandhills Nature Preserve.

ACKNOWLEDGMENTS

Grateful acknowledgment is made to the editors of the following publications, in which these poems, sometimes in very different forms, first appeared.

Academy of American Poets Poem-a-Day	"Letter Beginning with Two Lines by Czesław Miłosz"
	"Letter to Someone Living Fifty Years from Now"
Ampersand Review	"Letter to My Car's Radiator"
	"Letter to Steve Orlen—"
	"Letter to Jamaal May Regarding the Existence of Unicorns"
	"Psychopomp"
Barrow Street	"Letter to a Man Drowning in a Folktale"

Cherry Tree	"Wing Case"
	"The First Official Post Office of the American Colonies (1639)"
The Compass	"Letter to Jennifer Chang and Evan Rhodes Regarding a Variation in the Fabric of Time"
Cream City Review	"Letter to Matthew Olzmann from the Roman Empire"
	"Letter to Matthew Olzmann from a Traffic Light in Durham, North Carolina"
The Greensboro Review	"Letter to Matthew Olzmann from a Flying Saucer"
Hobart	"Fourteen Letters to a 52-Hertz Whale"
Inch	"Letter to a Bridge Made of Rope—"
Kenyon Review	"Return to Sender"
	"Letter to a Cockroach, Now Dead and Mixed into a Bar of Chocolate"
Linebreak	"Letter to the Horse You Rode in on"
Los Angeles Review of Books	"Letter to the Oldest Living Longleaf Pine in North America"
MacGuffin	"Letter to a Canyon"
	"Letter to Matthew Olzmann, Sent Telepathically from a Flock of Pigeons While

	Surrounding Him on a Park Bench in Detroit, Michigan"
Qualm	"Daylight Container"
Raleigh Review	"Phantom Route" "Day Zero"
Tin House	"Letter to the Person Who Carved His Initials into the Oldest Living Longleaf Pine in North America"
THRUSH	"The Dead Letter Office" "Letter to Larry Levis"
Virginia Quarterly Review	"Letter to Bruce Wayne"
Waxwing	"Letter Written While Waiting in Line at Comic Con" "Letter to the Person Who, During the Q&A Session after the Reading, Asked for Career Advice"
Water~Stone Review	"Letter to David James" "Conversion"

"Letter Beginning with Two Lines by Czeslaw Miłosz" also appeared in *Best American Poetry, 2017.*

"Letter to the Person Who, During the Q&A Session after the Reading, Asked for Career Advice" also appeared in *Best American Poetry, 2020.*

"Day Zero" also appeared in *The Orison Anthology, 2017.*

This next part might be really obvious, but:

"Letter to Matthew Olzmann from Cathy Linh Che on Saintlinesss" was written by Cathy Linh Che.
"Questions for Matthew Olzmann from Jessica Jacobs about Imposter Syndrome among the Thorns and Thistles" was written by Jessica Jacobs and first appeared in *Talking River.*
"Letter to Matthew Olzmann from Ross White, RE: The Tardigrade" was written by Ross White.
"Letter to Matthew Olzmann from Mike Scalise Concerning Love and Echoes" was written by Mike Scalise.
"Some Notes from Vievee on the Kindness of Shepherds" was written by Vievee Francis.
"Letter to Matthew Olzmann, Sent Telepathically from a Flock of Pigeons While Surrounding Him on a Park Bench in Detroit, Michigan" was written by a bunch of pigeons.

For their immense contributions, insights, and generosity of spirit: thank you to Kaveh Akbar, Dilruba Ahmed, Tommye Blount, Cathy Linh Che, Jessica Jacobs, David Tomas Martinez, Alicia Jo Rabins, Mike Scalise, and Ross White. Thank you to MacDowell for the gift of time and space needed to complete this book. Thank you to Carey Salerno, Alyssa Neptune, and everyone at Alice James Books. Lyrics N' Layups. The MFA Program for Writers at Warren Wilson College. Kundiman Forever.

A significant amount of gratitude is owed to David James who, nearly twenty years ago in a classroom at Oakland Community College, said: "Matthew, all poems are basically letters, especially yours."

Recent Titles from Alice James Books

Alice James Books is committed to publishing books that matter. The press was founded in 1973 in Boston, Massachusetts as a cooperative, wherein authors performed the day-to-day undertakings of the press. This element remains present today, as authors who publish with the press are invited to collaborate closely in the publication process of their work. AJB remains committed to its founders' original feminist mission, while expanding upon the scope to include all voices and poets who might otherwise go unheard. In keeping with its efforts to build equity and increase inclusivity in publishing and the literary arts, AJB seeks out poets whose writing possesses the range, depth, and ability to cultivate empathy in our world and to dynamically push against silence. The press was named for Alice James, sister to William and Henry, whose extraordinary gift for writing went unrecognized during her lifetime.

Designed by Tiani Kennedy

Printed by McNaughton & Gunn

CPSIA information can be obtained
at www.ICGtesting.com
Printed in the USA
JSHW012124130123
36274JS00005B/5